Contents

BROMLEY PUBLIC LIBRARIES

0233755531

Askews	u. 12.00
J7300 MOO	£4.99
	CHU

Who was Henry Moore?

Henry Moore was one of the most important
artists of this century. He made huge **sculptures**
out of stone, wood and **bronze**. He also made
many drawings.

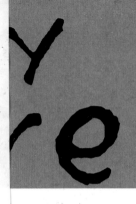

Leisure & Community Services

Please return this item by the last date stamped below, to the library from which it was borrowed.

Renewals

You may renew any item twice (for 3 weeks) by telephone or post, providing it is not required by another reader. *Please quote the number stated below.*

Overdue charges

Please see library notices for the current rate of charges for overdue items. Overdue charges are not made on junior books unless borrowed on adult tickets.

Postage

Both adult and junior borrowers must pay any postage on overdue notices.

5 FEB 2001	24/11/06 KME
	26 AUG 2008
17 APR 2001	20 OCT 2009
	3 1 MAY 2011
14 MAY 2001	3 1 MAY 2011
26 May SP	
20 MAR 2003	24 MAR 2012
13 NOV 2003	- 7 APR 2012
28 SEP 2004 3 NOV 2006	
	2 1 OCT 2012
	2 8 APR 2014 739.96

23 APR 2019   CHISLEHURST
020 8467 1318

N BOROUGH

Sean Connolly

Heinemann LIBRARY

BROMLEY LIBRARIES

3 0128 02337 5531

First published in Great Britain by
Heinemann Library,
Halley Court, Jordan Hill, Oxford OX2 8EJ
a division of Reed Educational and Professional
Publishing Ltd.
Heinemann is a registered trademark of Reed
Educational & Professional Publishing Ltd.

OXFORD MELBOURNE AUCKLAND
JOHANNESBURG BLANTYRE GABORONE
IBADAN PORTSMOUTH (NH) USA CHICAGO

© Reed Educational and Professional Publishing Ltd
2000
The moral right of the proprietor has been asserted.

All rights reserved. No part of this publication may
be reproduced, stored in a retrieval system, or
transmitted in any form or by any means,
electronic, mechanical, photocopying, recording, or
otherwise without either the prior written
permission of the Publishers or a licence permitting
restricted copying in the United Kingdom issued by
the Copyright Licensing Agency Ltd, 90 Tottenham
Court Road, London W1P 0LP.

Designed by Celia Floyd
Originated by Dot Gradations
Printed in Hong Kong/China

04 03 02 01 00
10 9 8 7 6 5 4 3 2 1

ISBN 0 431 09187 0
This title is also available in a hardback library
edition (ISBN 0 431 09179 X).

British Library Cataloguing in Publication Data

Connolly, Sean
    Life and work of Henry Moore
    1. Moore, Henry, 1898-1986 – Juvenile literature
    2. Artists – England – Biography – Juvenile literature
    3. Art, Modern – 20th century – England – Juvenile
    literature
    I. Title
    730.9'2

For more information about Heinemann Library
books, or to order, please telephone
+44(0)1865 888066, or send a fax to +441865 314091.
You can visit our web site at www.heinemann.co.uk

Acknowledgements

The Publishers would like to thank the following for
permission to reproduce photographs:

The Henry Moore Foundation for:

Page 4, 'Portrait Studio, 1960'. Page 5, Henry
Moore 'Three Forms: Vertebrae'. Page 6, Henry
Moore aged 11. Page 7, Castleford Grammar
School's Roll of Honour. Page 8, Henry Moore
convalescing at Castleford Grammar School, 1918.
Page 9, Henry Moore 'Small Animal Head 1921'.
Page 10, Corner of Studio Adie Road 1928. Page 11,
Henry Moore 'Reclining Figure 1929'. Page 12,
Henry Moore with West Wind 1928. Page 13, North
wall of Headquarters of London Underground.
Page 14, Corner of studio at 11a Parkhill Road
Hampstead 1936. Page 15, Henry Moore 'Reclining
Figure 1936'. Page 17, Henry Moore 'Two forms
1934'. Page 18, Lee Miller, Henry Moore in Holborn
Underground, London 1943. Page 19, Henry Moore
'Pink and Green Sleepers 1941'. Page 20, Lee Miller
Archives, Henry Moore with Severini in Venice for
the Biennale 1948. Page 21, Henry Moore
'Madonna and child'. Page 22, Henry Moore
carving UNESCO Reclining Figure 1957-58. Page 23
Henry Moore 'Draped Reclining Figure 1952-53'.
Page 24, Henry Moore in Top Studio 1954. Page 25,
Henry Moore 'Double Oval'. Page 26, Henry Moore
working in new maquette studio 1978. Page 27,
Henry Moore 'Sheep Piece 1962-63'. Page 28, The
Independent. Page 29, Henry Moore 'Large Figure
in a shelter 1952-53'.

Page 16, Robert Harding Picture Library.

Cover photograph reproduced with permission of
Bridgeman Art library

Our thanks to Paul Flux for his comments in the
preparation of this book and to Emma Stower at
the Henry Moore Foundation for all her help with
the picture selection.

Every effort has been made to contact copyright
holders of any material reproduced in this book.
Any omissions will be rectified in subsequent
printings if notice is given to the Publisher.

Any words appearing in the text in bold, **like this**,
are explained in the Glossary.

People from around the world asked Henry to make sculptures for them. This sculpture, made in 1978, stands in Dallas, USA.

Early years

Henry Moore was born on 30 July 1898 in Castleford, England. His father was a **miner**. When Henry was 12 years old he won a **scholarship** to Castleford Grammar School.

Henry was already good at art. When he was 16 years old his teachers asked him to **carve** this **roll of honour** for the school.

London

Henry fought in the **First World War** for two years. In 1921 he began studying at the Royal College of Art in London. Two years later he visited Paris.

Henry saw many types of art in London and Paris. Henry made this **sculpture** of a small animal head in London in 1921.

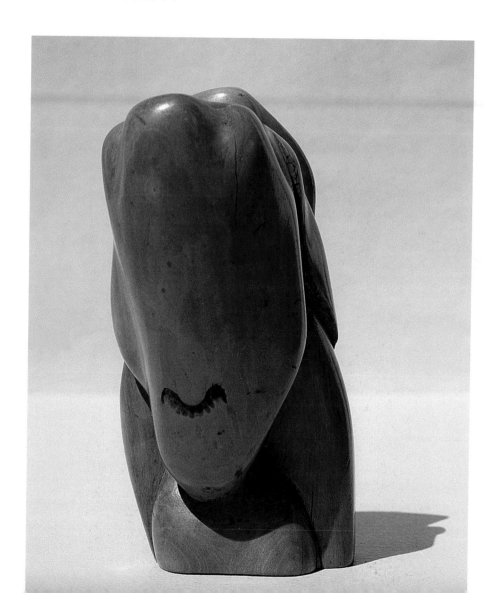

Settling in

In 1925 Henry became a teacher at the Royal College of Art in London. He was also busy making his own **sculptures**. In 1928 he had a one-man **exhibition** in London.

Henry **carved** his sculptures out of stone. He liked to show people lying on their side. He made many more sculptures like this one.

The public eye

Henry became more famous. When he was 31 he did his first **commission**. It was a huge **sculpture** for the London Underground.

The title of this sculpture was *The North Wind*. It shows Henry's interest in stone, fire, water and wind.

The modern world

In the 1930s Henry became interested in **abstract art**. His **sculpture** began to look less like human beings and more like simple, rounded shapes.

Henry collected pebbles, stones and shells to see how Nature creates shapes. This statue shows Henry's interest in smooth, curved surfaces.

Getting known

More and more people saw the beauty in Henry's large **sculptures**. They were **exhibited** in Europe and the USA. This is a picture of the Museum of Modern Art in New York, USA.

Henry sold this sculpture to the Museum of Modern Art in New York, USA. It shows how his sculptures were only partly **abstract**. Here you can still see human shapes.

War artist

The **Second World War** began in 1939. Two years later Henry was asked to become an official war artist. He drew the daily life of people in London during the war.

These drawings are some of Henry's most powerful works. This one shows people trying to sleep while bombs explode outside.

Travelling the world

After the war Henry travelled to many places. He got many awards and prizes for his **sculptures**. This picture shows Henry and a friend in Venice, Italy.

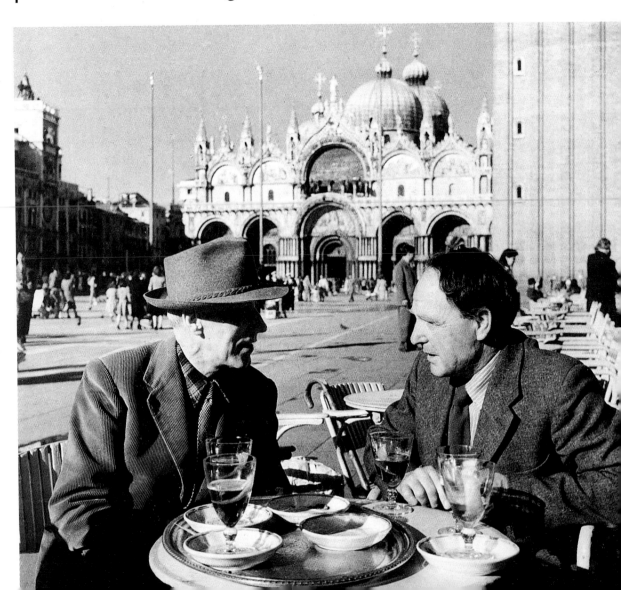

Henry's prizes did not change his way of thinking. He made this **tender** sculpture of Mary and Jesus for a church in Suffolk.

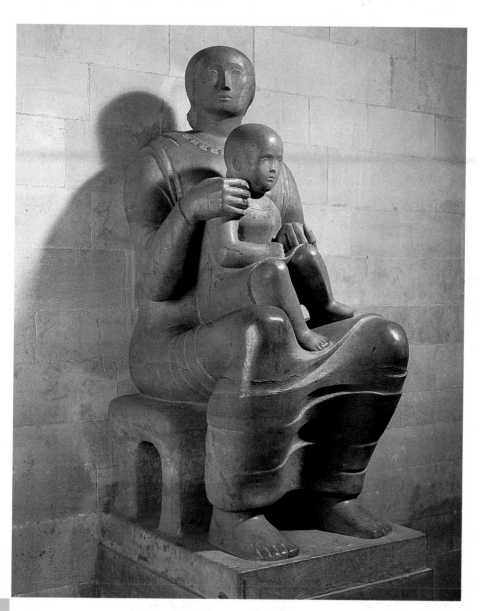

Time for a change

In the 1950s Henry tried new ways of working. Until then he **carved** directly from stone. Now he made many **sculptures** from **bronze** and wood.

Henry could make even bigger, smoother
sculptures out of bronze. This sculpture of a
woman is in front of a building in London.

New ideas

Henry also looked for new ideas. In the 1960s he began putting one shape inside another one. Many of these combined shapes created **hollow sculptures**.

Henry wanted people to look at his large sculptures from all sides. These two oval shapes seem alike at first. They only look different when you walk around them.

The sculptor's studio

Henry moved to Perry Green in Hertfordshire when London was bombed during the war. He was very happy there.

Sheep **grazed** in the field outside Henry's **studio**. In the 1970s Henry made many sketches of the sheep. He made this sculpture to go in the field.

An active life ends

Henry still worked when he was more than 80 years old. A special service in Westminster Abbey honoured Henry after his death on 31 August 1986.

Mourning Henry Moore yesterday: Jeremy Thorpe; Lord Snowdon and Sir Hugh Casson; Moore's daughter Mary Danowski and her children; Michael Foot and his wife, Jill Craigie.

Friends pay tribute to Moore

FELLOW ARTISTS and friends of the sculptor Henry Moore paid their last respects at a memorial service in Westminster Abbey yesterday. Many of his surviving contemporaries including his widow, Irina, whom he married in 1929, were too frail to attend.

Sir Stephen Spender, the poet, told the congregation that Moore, who died in August, aged 88, was the seventh son of a Yorkshire miner who never considered anyone either socially superior or inferior to himself.

Sir Stephen, one of the last surviving members of Moore's avant-garde Hampstead artistic circle in the Thirties, delivered the address in a brisk, husky whisper. He remembered Moore's studio as a focal point for artists, including Ben Nicholson, the painter, and Barbara Hepworth, the sculptress.

He said that despite Moore's admiration for the abstract artists around him, "he told me he could never make an artefact which referred to nothing but itself".

Moore had confided to him: "Try as I might, my work always ended up looking like something, probably a reclining figure."

Sir Stephen quoted Sir Herbert Read, the poet and art critic, and a champion of Moore in the Thirties, saying that in his opinion the sculptor would have been the best possible ambassador from this planet to another.

Sir Stephen said: "He was an artist of great ingenuity and a man of great humanity." Moore had never forgotten the simplicity of his upbringing.

Dame Peggy Ashcroft, the actress, read the first lesson, not from the Bible but from the Apocrypha, the second book of Esdras. It concluded: "He who made all things, and searcheth out hidden things in hidden places, surely he knoweth your imagination, and what ye think in your hearts." The text was suggested to the Moore family by Westminster Abbey, because its words were so appropriate.

The second lesson, read by the Duke of Gloucester, was from Revelations, in the King James version, chosen because it is the one familiar to Moore's generation.

The congregation included the Prime Minister; Michael Foot, the former Labour leader; Sir Hugh Casson, the architect and painter; Sir Roy Strong, director of the Victoria and Albert Museum; Jeremy Thorpe, the former Liberal leader; John Profumo, the former Conservative Cabinet minister, Lord Snowdon and Sam Wanamaker, the film maker.

List of mourners, page 13